W9-CPM-808

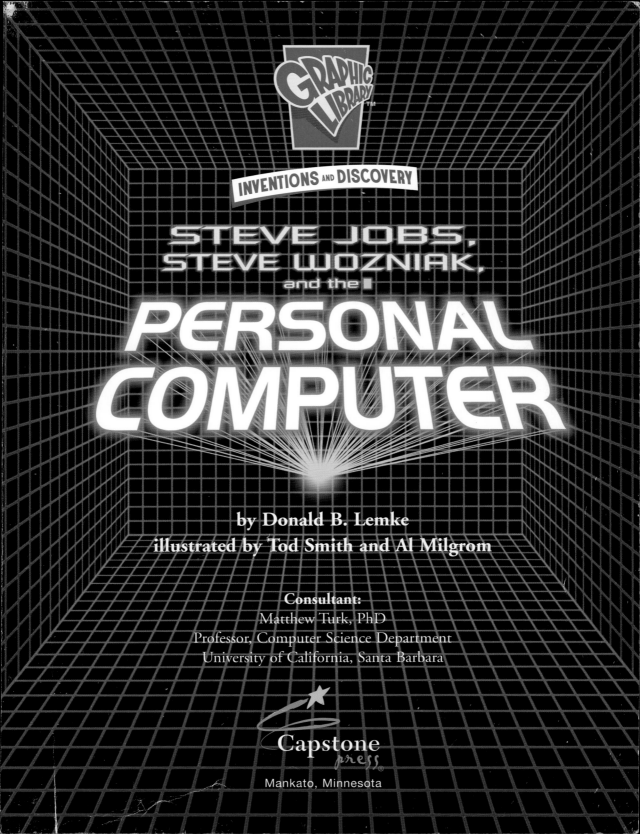

GRAPHIC LIBRARY™

INVENTIONS AND DISCOVERY

STEVE JOBS, STEVE WOZNIAK, and the

PERSONAL COMPUTER

by Donald B. Lemke

illustrated by Tod Smith and Al Milgrom

Consultant:
Matthew Turk, PhD
Professor, Computer Science Department
University of California, Santa Barbara

Capstone
press®

Mankato, Minnesota

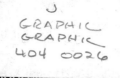

Graphic L[illegible] one Press,
151 Good Counsel D[illegible] o, Minnesota 56002.
www.capstonep[illegible]

Printed in the United States of America

1 2 3 4 5 6 11 10 09 08 07 06

Library of Congress Cataloging-in-Publication Data

Lemke, Donald B.

Steve Jobs, Steve Wozniak, and the personal computer / by Donald B. Lemke; illustrated by Tod Smith and Al Milgrom.

p. cm.—(Graphic library. Inventions and discovery)

Summary: "In graphic novel format, tells the story of how Steve Jobs and Steve Wozniak developed the personal computer"—Provided by publisher.

Includes bibliographical references and index.

ISBN-13: 978-0-7368-6488-6 (hardcover)
ISBN-10: 0-7368-6488-1 (hardcover)
ISBN-13: 978-0-7368-9650-4 (softcover pbk.)
ISBN-10: 0-7368-9650-3 (softcover pbk.)

1. Jobs, Steven, 1955– —Juvenile literature. 2. Wozniak, Stephen Gary, 1950– —Juvenile literature. 3. Computer engineers—United States—Biography—Juvenile literature. 4. Apple Computer, Inc.—History—Juvenile literature. I. Title. II. Series.

QA76.2.A2L48 2007
621.39092—dc22
[B] 2006011109

Designer
Bob Lentz

Colorist
Otha Zackariah Edward Lohse

Editor
Christopher Harbo

Editor's note: Direct quotations from primary sources are indicated by a yellow background.

Direct quotations appear on the following pages:
Page 26, from Steve Jobs' speech on January 24, 1984, as archived on Mac Essentials (http://www.mac-essentials.de/index.php/mac/14276).

TABLE OF CONTENTS

CHAPTER 1

THE TWO STEVES

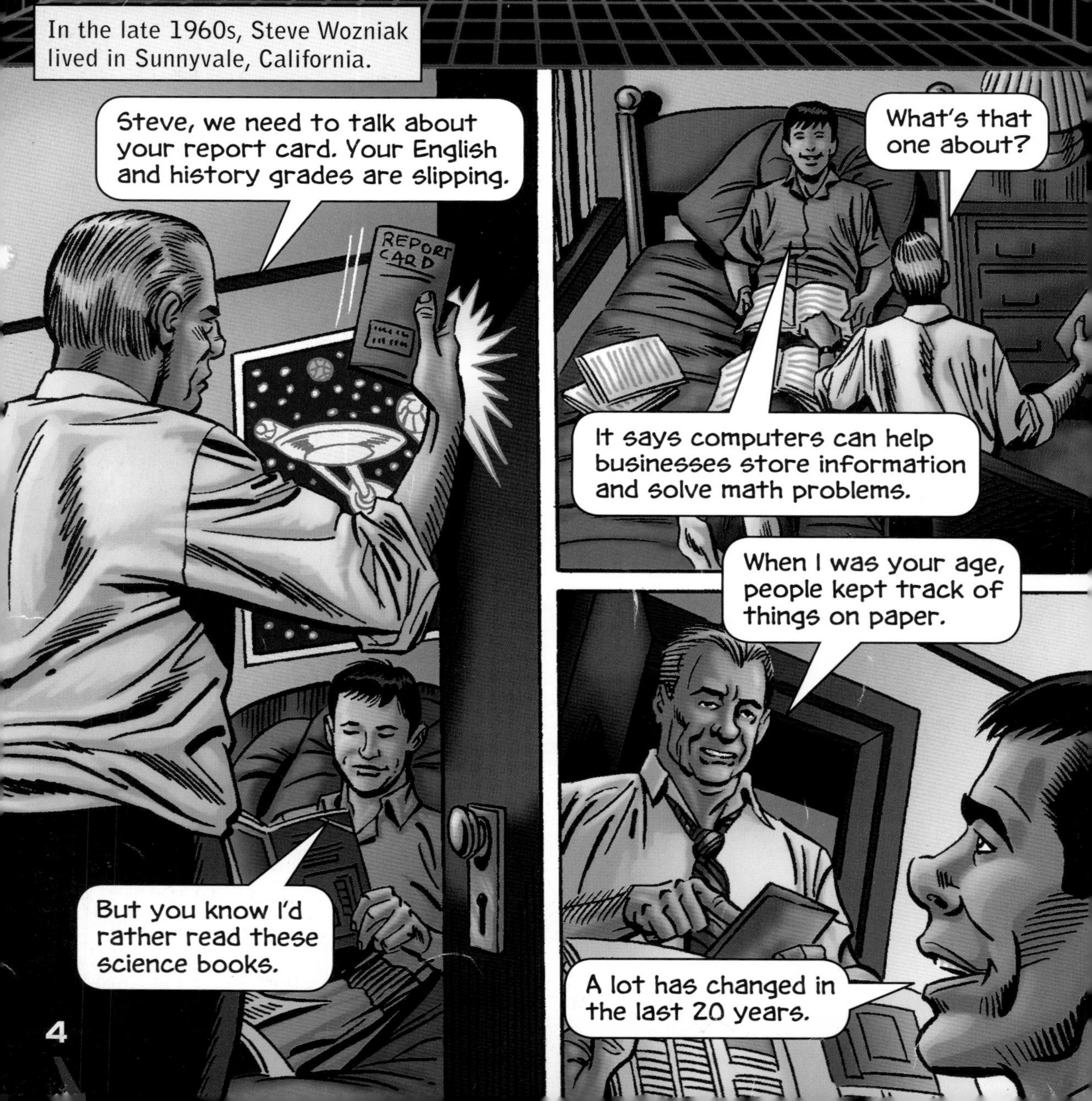

In the late 1960s, Steve Wozniak lived in Sunnyvale, California.
Steve, we need to talk about your report card. Your English and history grades are slipping.
REPORT CARD
But you know I'd rather read these science books.
What's that one about?
It says computers can help businesses store information and solve math problems.
When I was your age, people kept track of things on paper.
A lot has changed in the last 20 years.

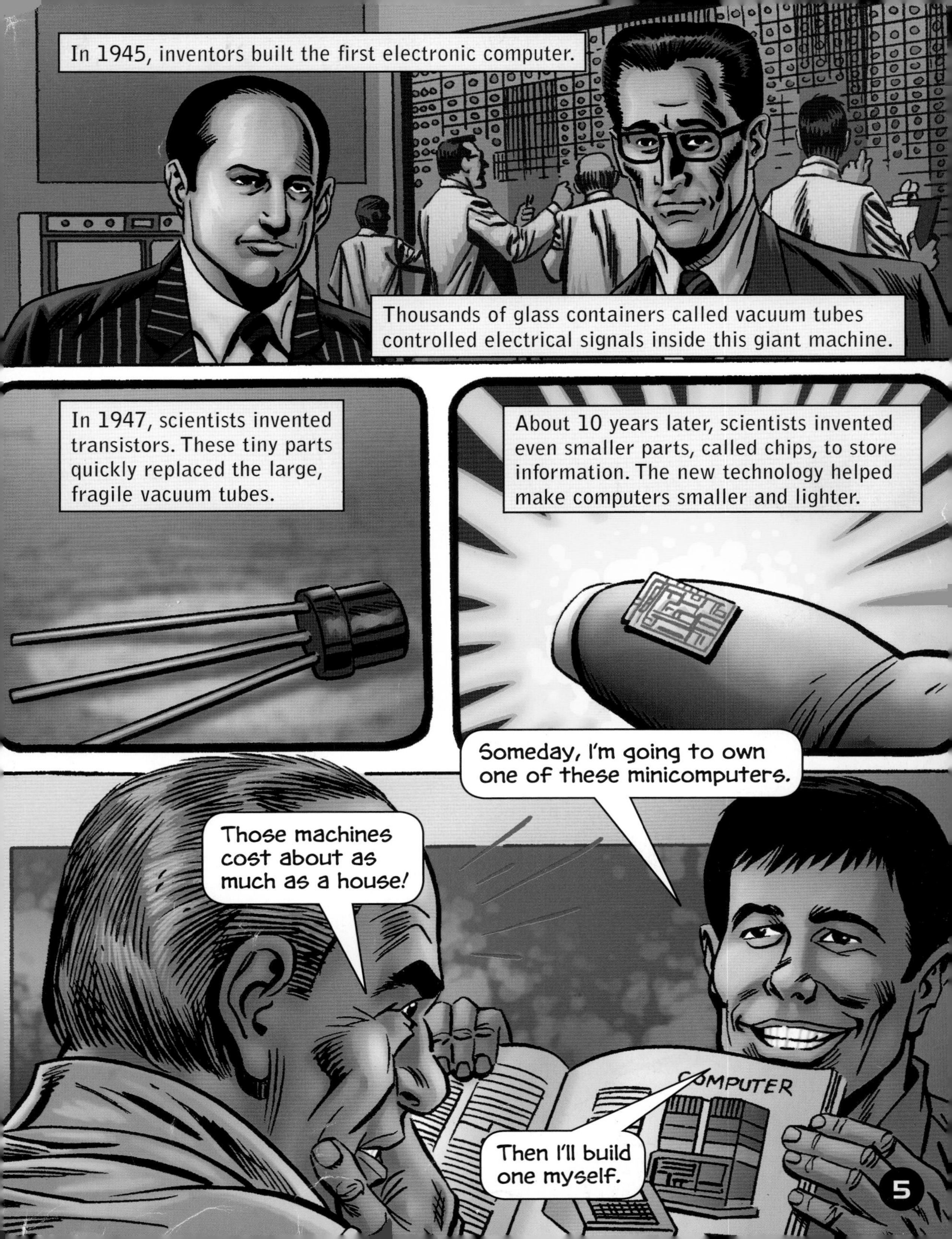
In 1945, inventors built the first electronic computer.
Thousands of glass containers called vacuum tubes controlled electrical signals inside this giant machine.
In 1947, scientists invented transistors. These tiny parts quickly replaced the large, fragile vacuum tubes.
About 10 years later, scientists invented even smaller parts, called chips, to store information. The new technology helped make computers smaller and lighter.
Someday, I'm going to own one of these minicomputers.
Those machines cost about as much as a house!
Then I'll build one myself.
COMPUTER

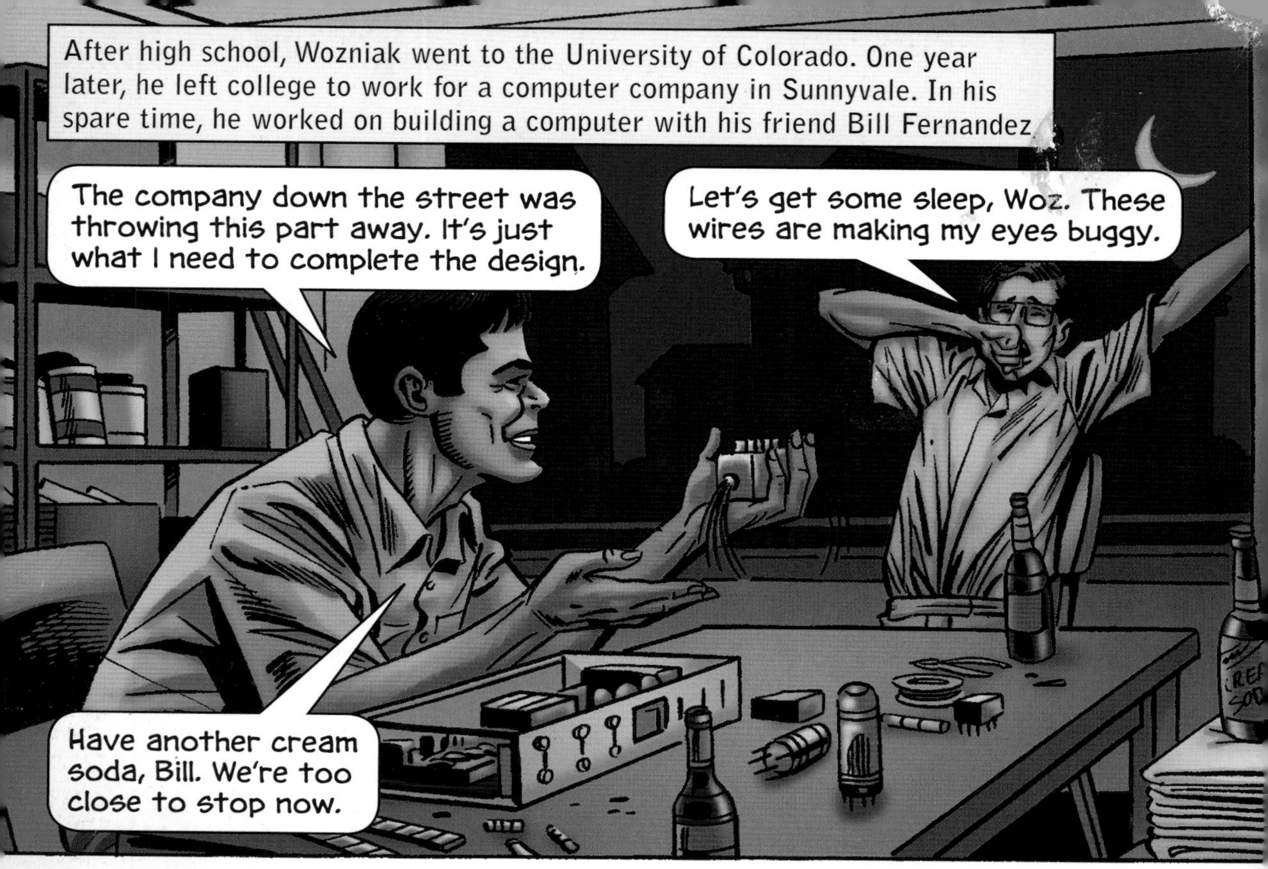
After high school, Wozniak went to the University of Colorado. One year later, he left college to work for a computer company in Sunnyvale. In his spare time, he worked on building a computer with his friend Bill Fernandez.
The company down the street was throwing this part away. It's just what I need to complete the design.
Let's get some sleep, Woz. These wires are making my eyes buggy.
Have another cream soda, Bill. We're too close to stop now.

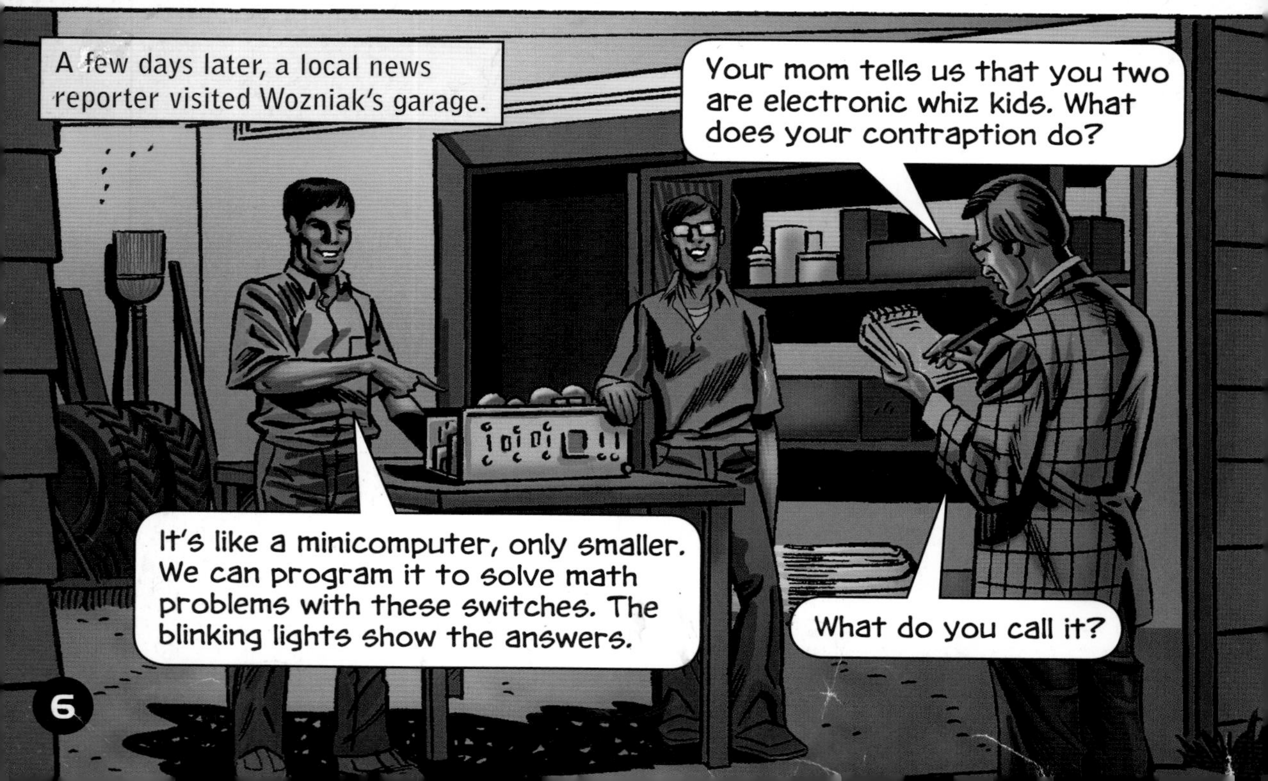
A few days later, a local news reporter visited Wozniak's garage.
Your mom tells us that you two are electronic whiz kids. What does your contraption do?
It's like a minicomputer, only smaller. We can program it to solve math problems with these switches. The blinking lights show the answers.
What do you call it?

The Cream Soda Computer.

KLIKK

CREAM SODA
FRAGMONT

FFZZZZLLL!

Well, it sure does fizzle like soda pop!

Maybe you boys should find a new hobby.

Why are you laughing? This thing could have made us famous.

I had fun just building it. We'll make something better tomorrow.

CREAM SODA   CREAM SODA

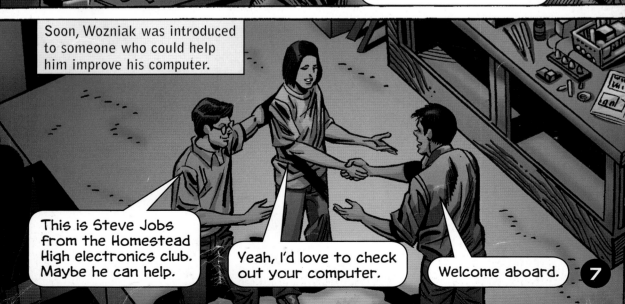

Soon, Wozniak was introduced to someone who could help him improve his computer.

This is Steve Jobs from the Homestead High electronics club. Maybe he can help.

Yeah, I'd love to check out your computer.

Welcome aboard.

7

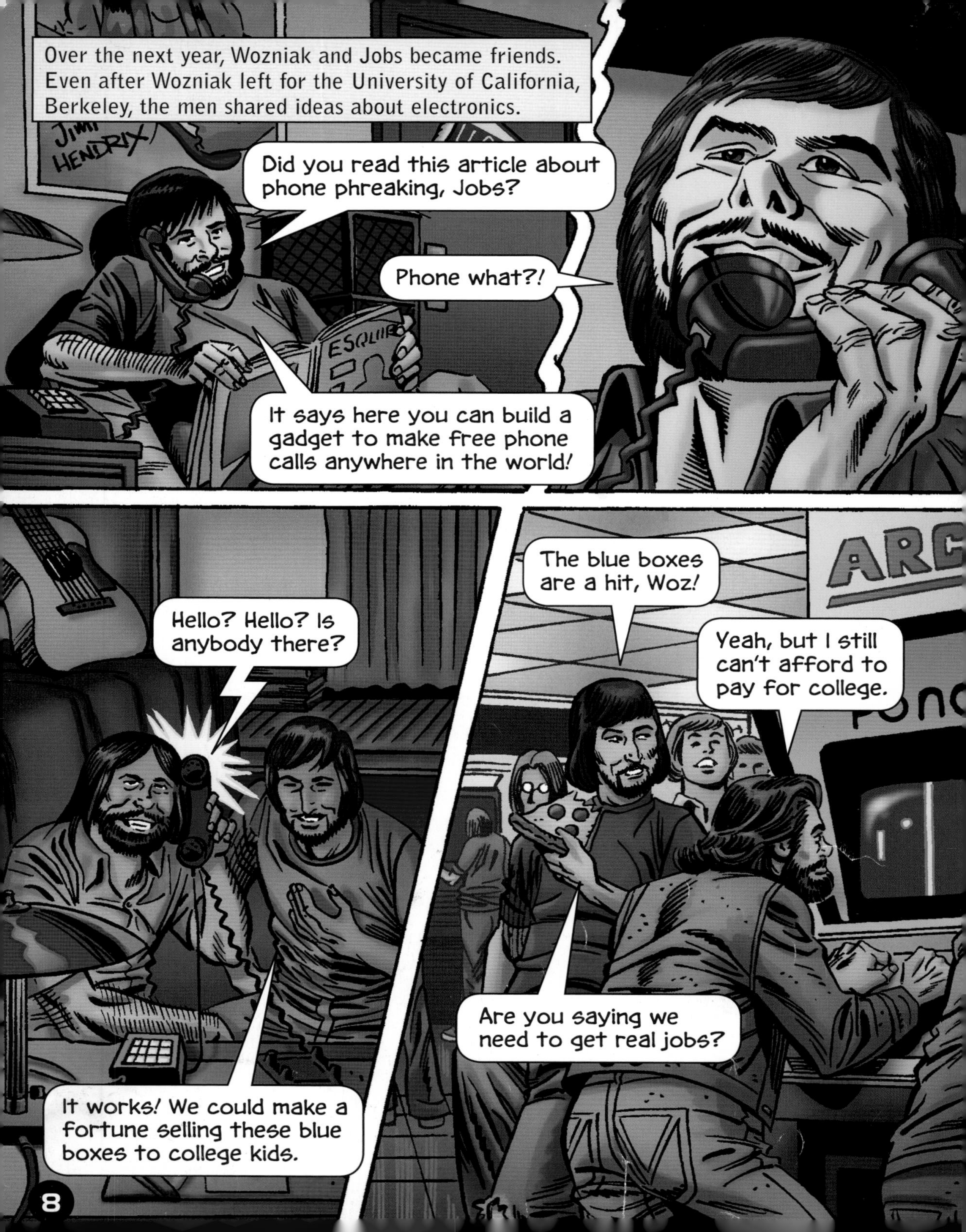
Over the next year, Wozniak and Jobs became friends. Even after Wozniak left for the University of California, Berkeley, the men shared ideas about electronics.
JIMI HENDRIX
Did you read this article about phone phreaking, Jobs?
Phone what?!
It says here you can build a gadget to make free phone calls anywhere in the world!
Hello? Hello? Is anybody there?
It works! We could make a fortune selling these blue boxes to college kids.
The blue boxes are a hit, Woz!
Yeah, but I still can't afford to pay for college.
Are you saying we need to get real jobs?

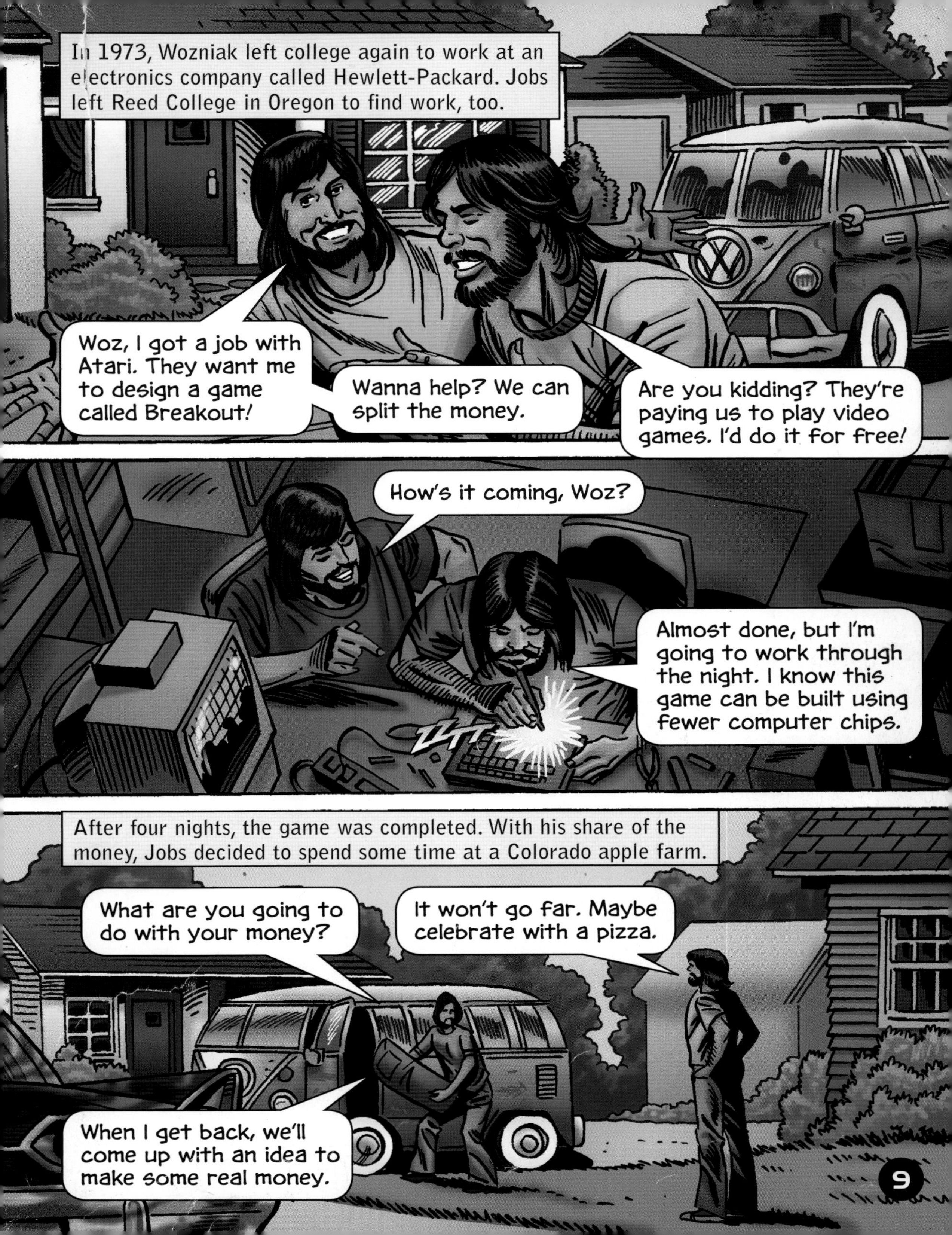
In 1973, Wozniak left college again to work at an electronics company called Hewlett-Packard. Jobs left Reed College in Oregon to find work, too.
Woz, I got a job with Atari. They want me to design a game called Breakout!
Wanna help? We can split the money.
Are you kidding? They're paying us to play video games. I'd do it for free!
How's it coming, Woz?
Almost done, but I'm going to work through the night. I know this game can be built using fewer computer chips.
After four nights, the game was completed. With his share of the money, Jobs decided to spend some time at a Colorado apple farm.
What are you going to do with your money?
It won't go far. Maybe celebrate with a pizza.
When I get back, we'll come up with an idea to make some real money.

CHAPTER 2 | DISCOVERING APPLE

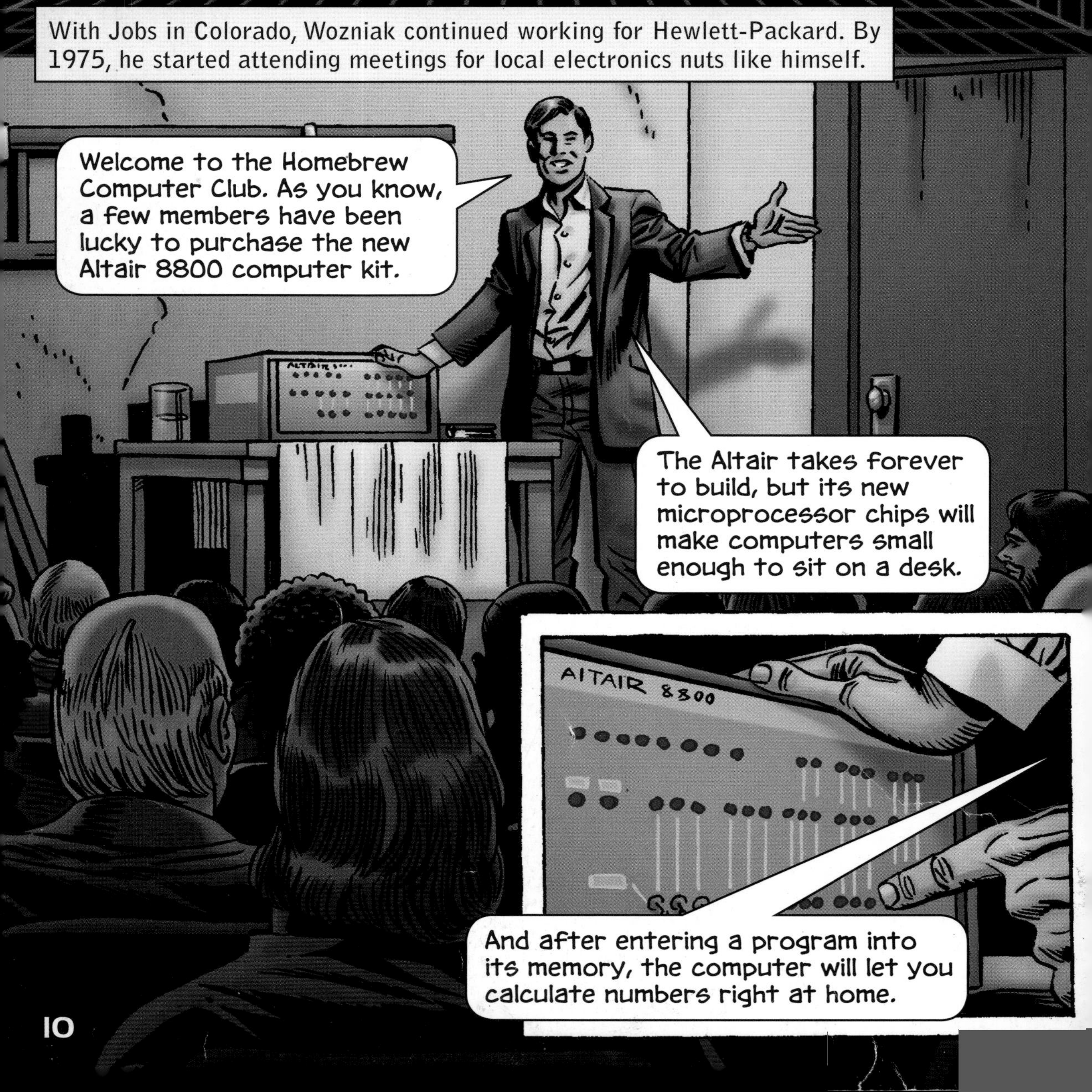
With Jobs in Colorado, Wozniak continued working for Hewlett-Packard. By 1975, he started attending meetings for local electronics nuts like himself.
Welcome to the Homebrew Computer Club. As you know, a few members have been lucky to purchase the new Altair 8800 computer kit.
The Altair takes forever to build, but its new microprocessor chips will make computers small enough to sit on a desk.
ALTAIR 8800
And after entering a program into its memory, the computer will let you calculate numbers right at home.

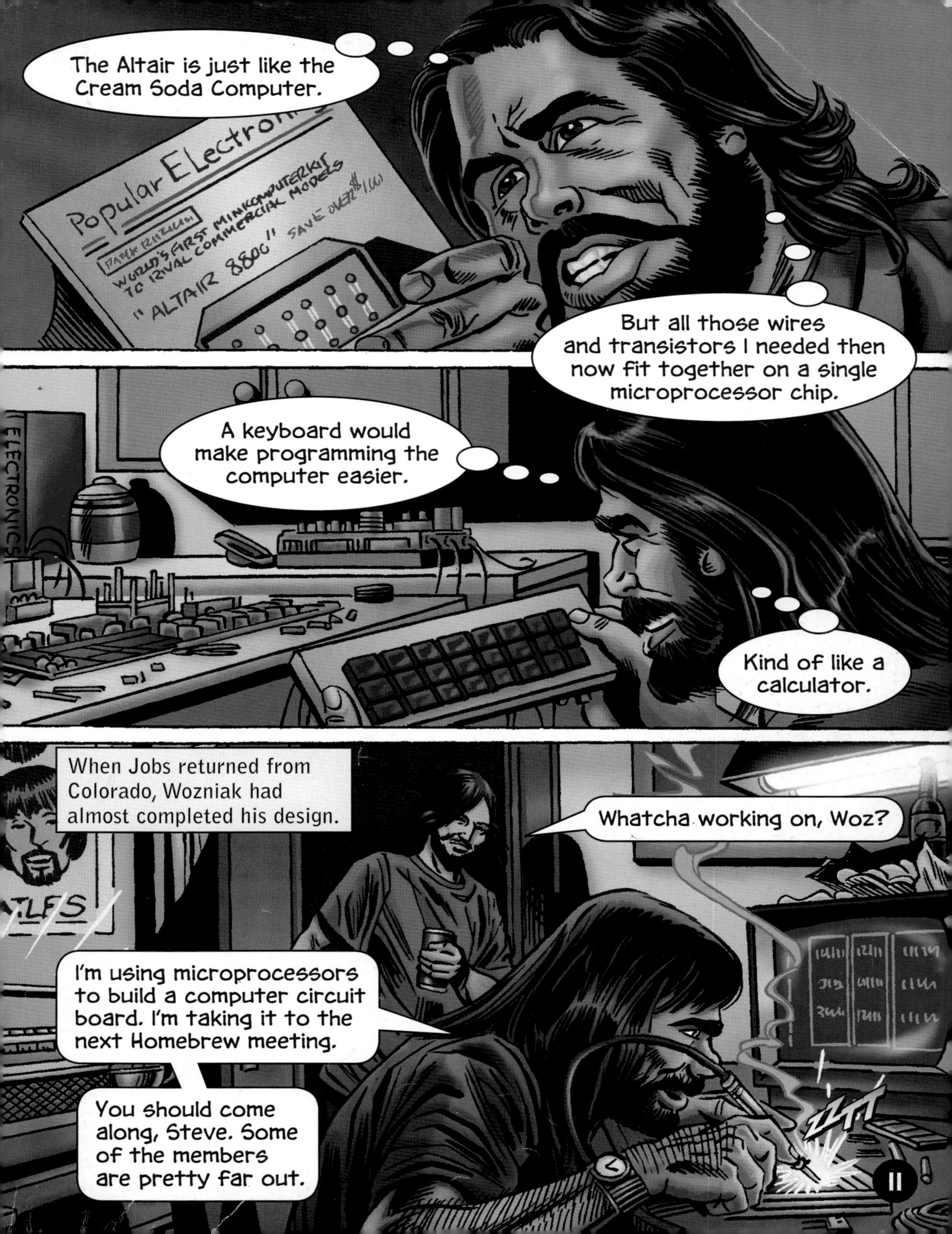
The Altair is just like the Cream Soda Computer.
Popular Electronics
"ALTAIR 8800"
But all those wires and transistors I needed then now fit together on a single microprocessor chip.
ELECTRONICS
A keyboard would make programming the computer easier.
Kind of like a calculator.
When Jobs returned from Colorado, Wozniak had almost completed his design.
Whatcha working on, Woz?
I'm using microprocessors to build a computer circuit board. I'm taking it to the next Homebrew meeting.
You should come along, Steve. Some of the members are pretty far out.

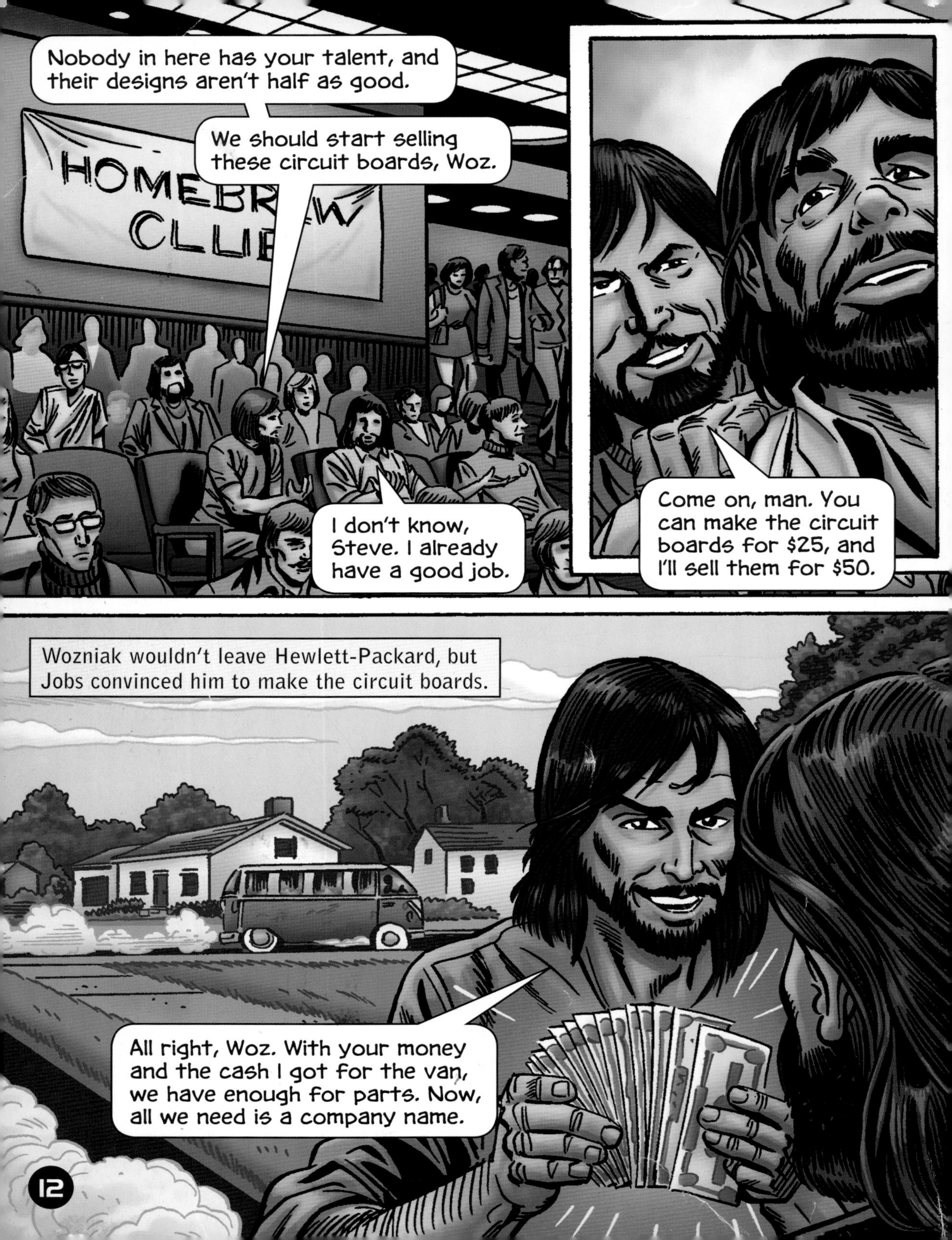
HOMEBREW CLUB
Nobody in here has your talent, and their designs aren't half as good.
We should start selling these circuit boards, Woz.
I don't know, Steve. I already have a good job.
Come on, man. You can make the circuit boards for $25, and I'll sell them for $50.
Wozniak wouldn't leave Hewlett-Packard, but Jobs convinced him to make the circuit boards.
All right, Woz. With your money and the cash I got for the van, we have enough for parts. Now, all we need is a company name.

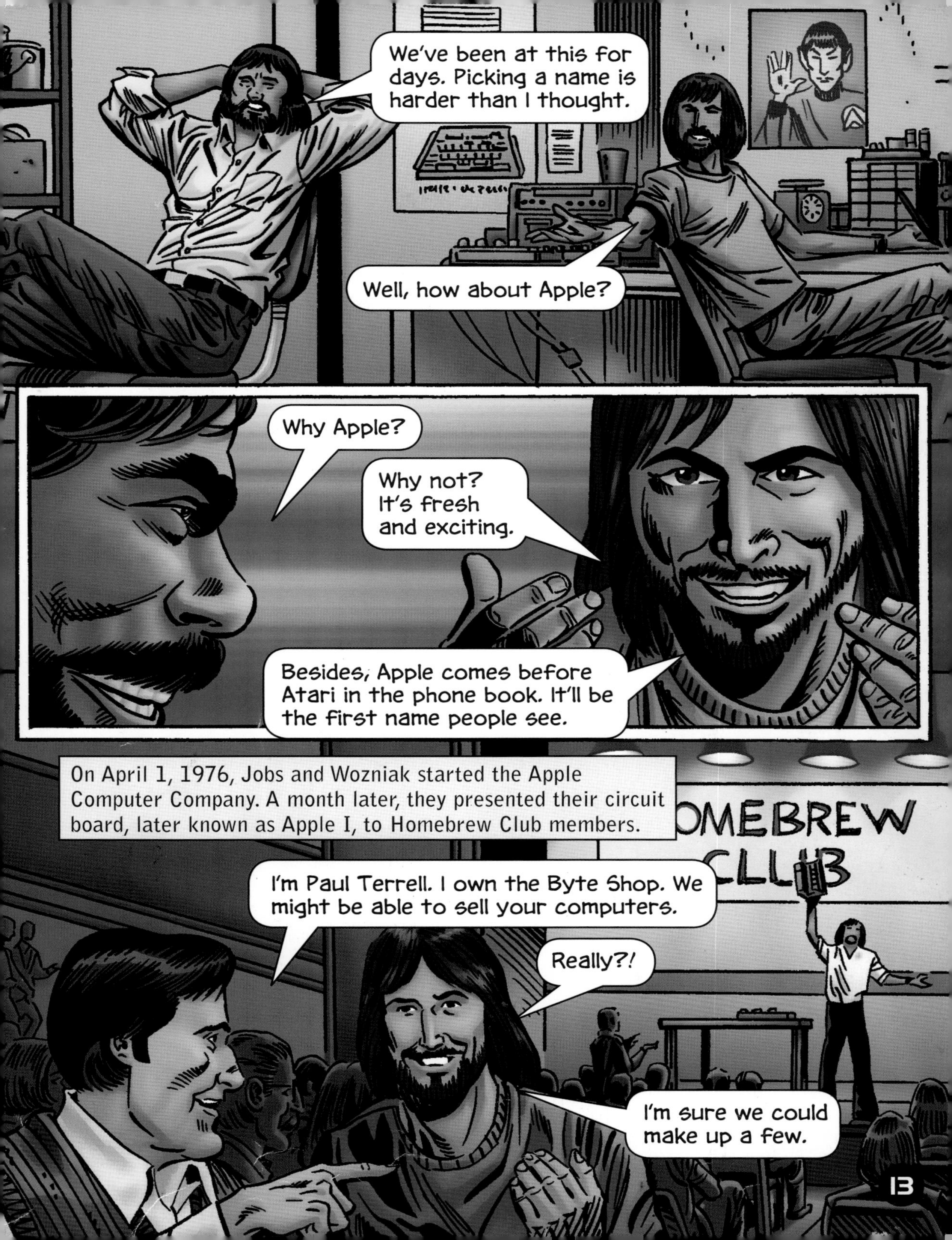
We've been at this for days. Picking a name is harder than I thought.
Well, how about Apple?
Why Apple?
Why not? It's fresh and exciting.
Besides, Apple comes before Atari in the phone book. It'll be the first name people see.
On April 1, 1976, Jobs and Wozniak started the Apple Computer Company. A month later, they presented their circuit board, later known as Apple I, to Homebrew Club members.
OMEBREW CLUB
I'm Paul Terrell. I own the Byte Shop. We might be able to sell your computers.
Really?!
I'm sure we could make up a few.

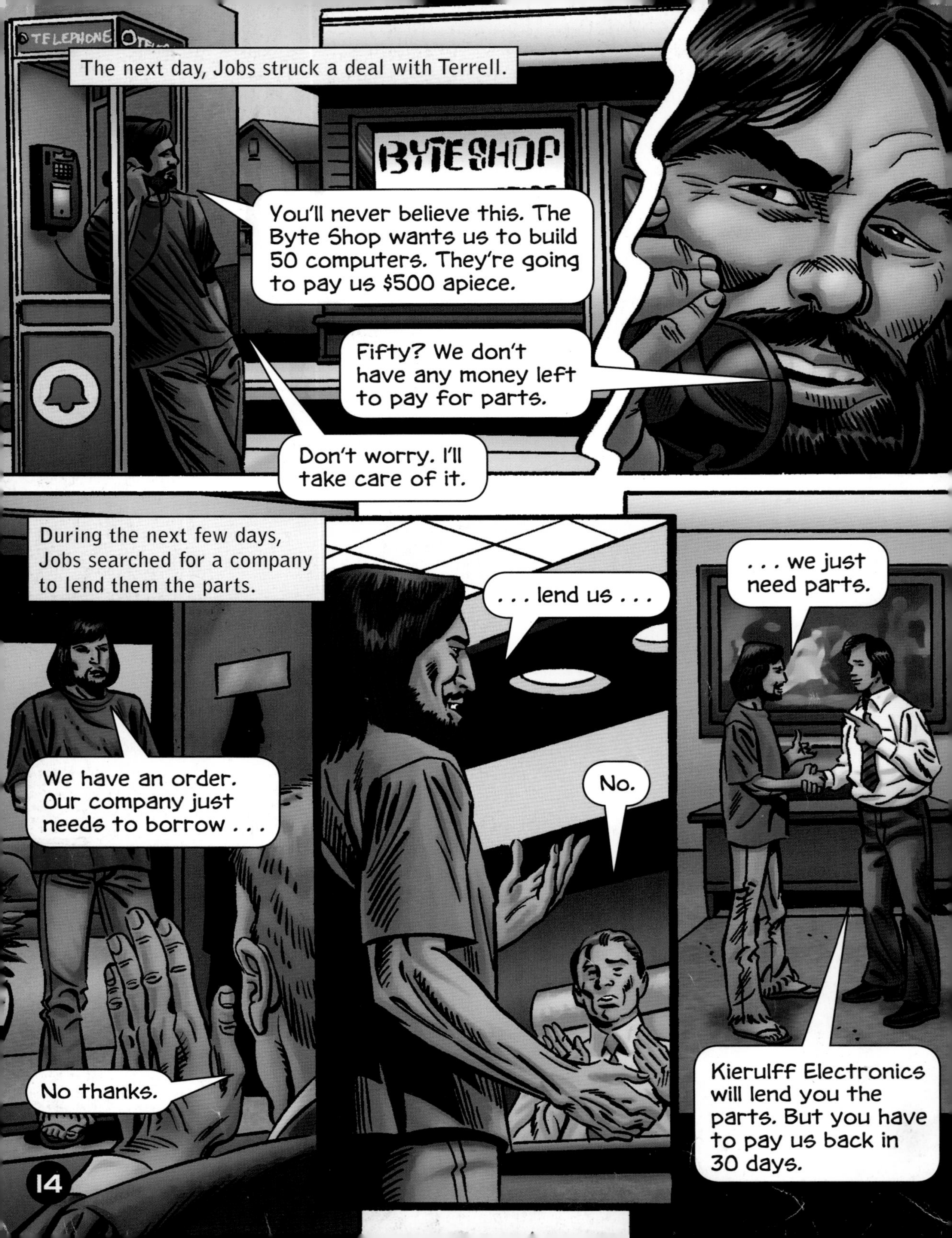

TELEPHONE
The next day, Jobs struck a deal with Terrell.
BYTE SHOP
You'll never believe this. The Byte Shop wants us to build 50 computers. They're going to pay us $500 apiece.
Fifty? We don't have any money left to pay for parts.
Don't worry. I'll take care of it.
During the next few days, Jobs searched for a company to lend them the parts.
We have an order. Our company just needs to borrow . . .
No thanks.
. . . lend us . . .
No.
. . . we just need parts.
Kierulff Electronics will lend you the parts. But you have to pay us back in 30 days.

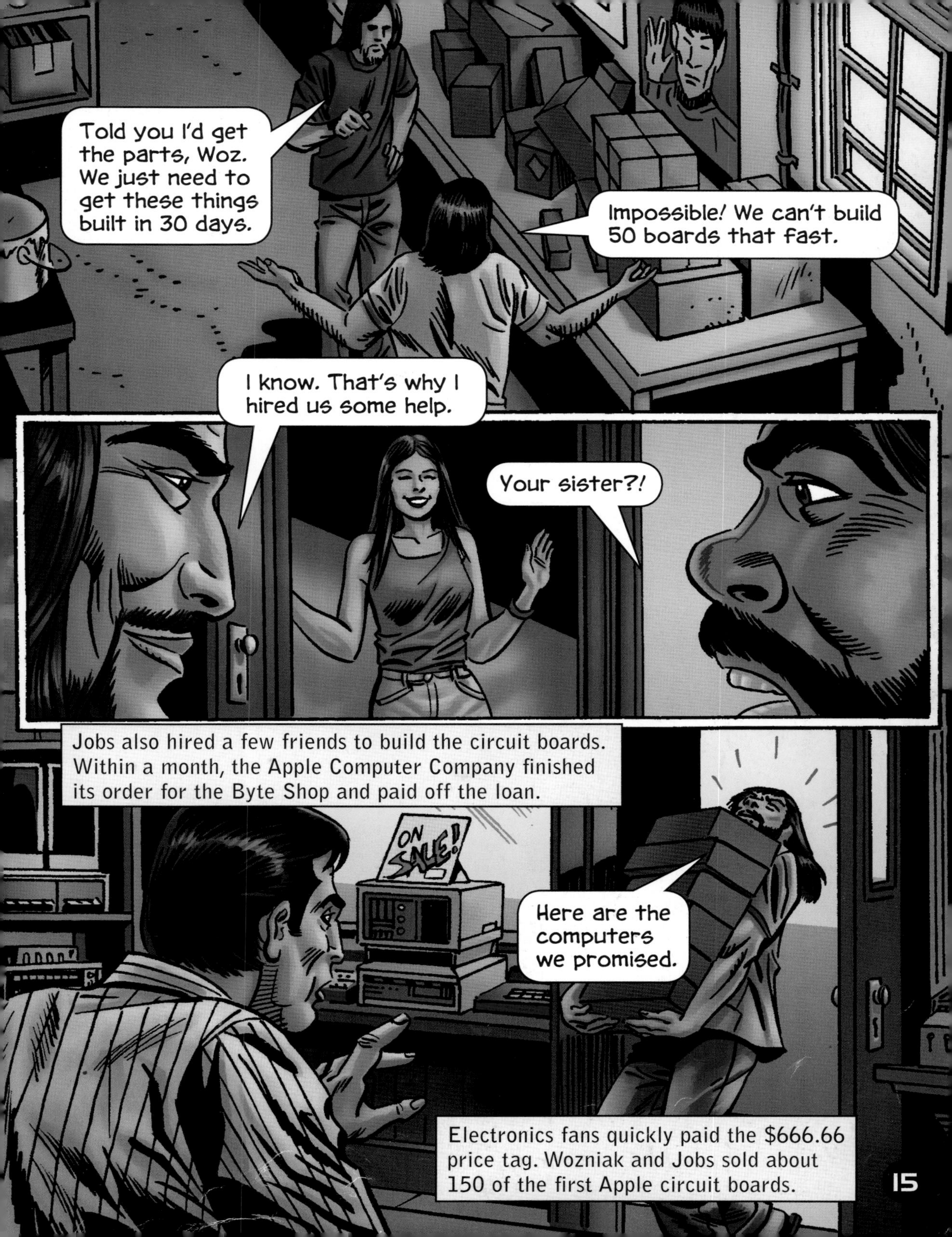
Told you I'd get the parts, Woz. We just need to get these things built in 30 days.
Impossible! We can't build 50 boards that fast.
I know. That's why I hired us some help.
Your sister?!
Jobs also hired a few friends to build the circuit boards. Within a month, the Apple Computer Company finished its order for the Byte Shop and paid off the loan.
ON SALE!
Here are the computers we promised.
Electronics fans quickly paid the $666.66 price tag. Wozniak and Jobs sold about 150 of the first Apple circuit boards.

CHAPTER 3: SELLING APPLES

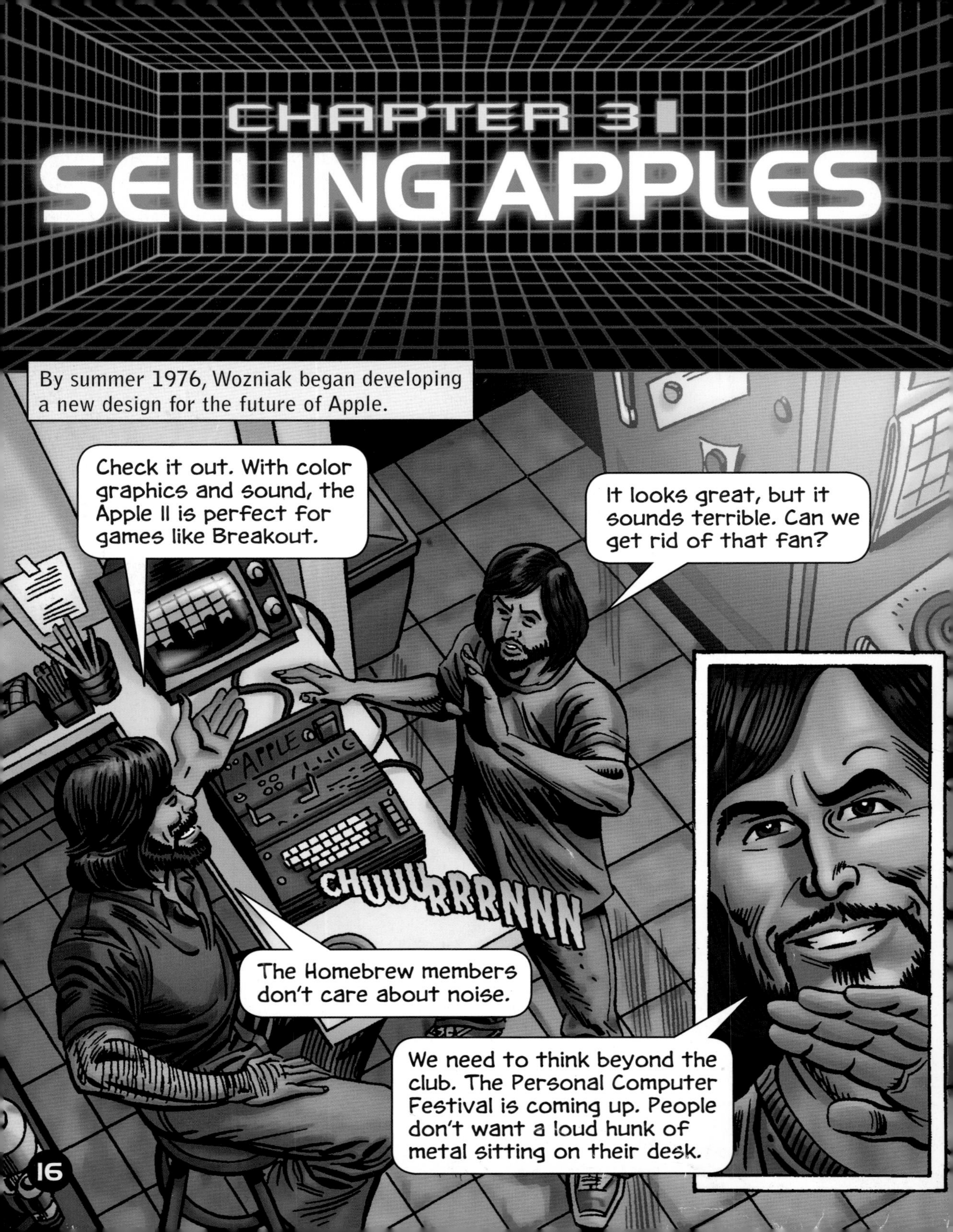
By summer 1976, Wozniak began developing a new design for the future of Apple.
Check it out. With color graphics and sound, the Apple II is perfect for games like Breakout.
It looks great, but it sounds terrible. Can we get rid of that fan?
CHUUURRRNNN
The Homebrew members don't care about noise.
We need to think beyond the club. The Personal Computer Festival is coming up. People don't want a loud hunk of metal sitting on their desk.

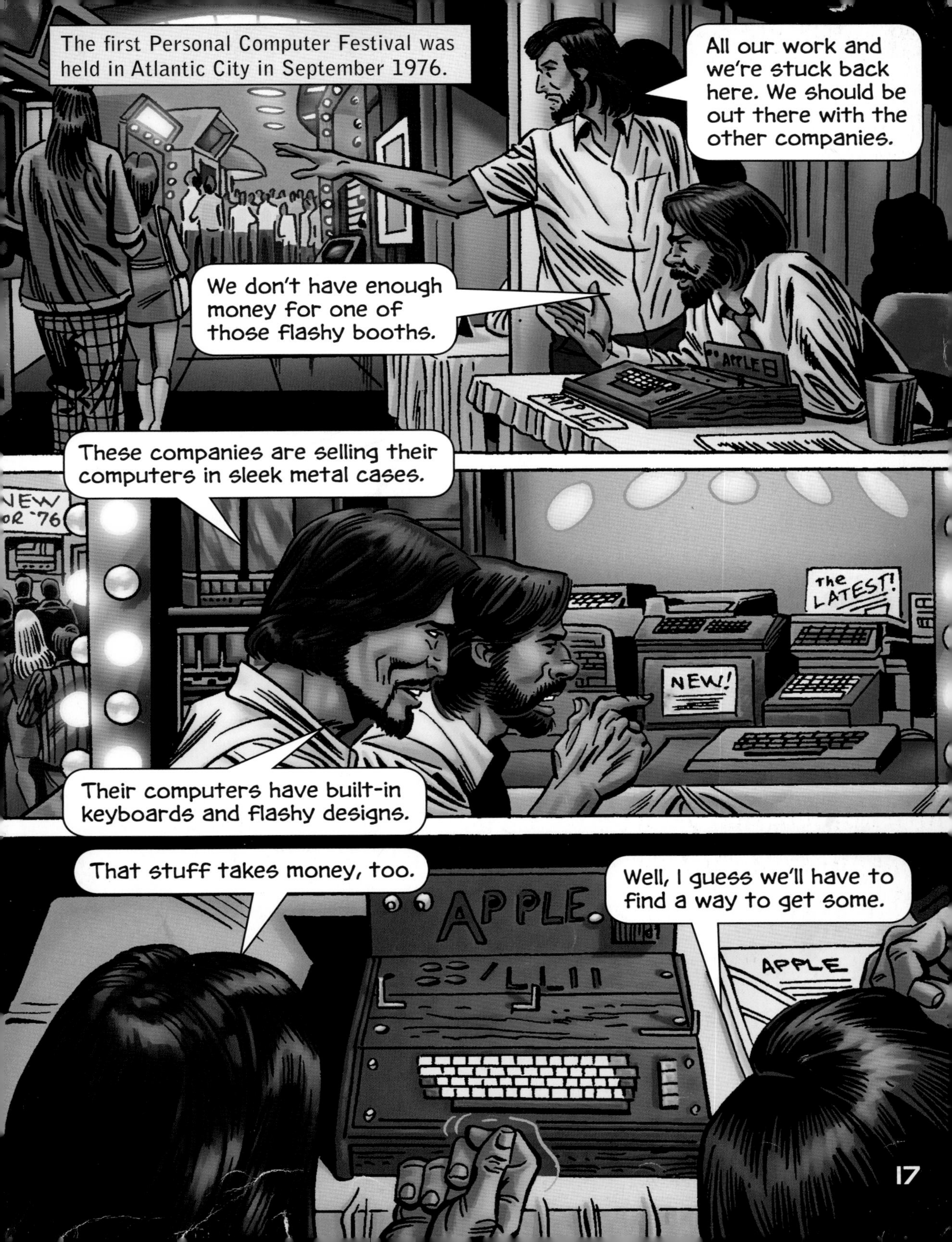
The first Personal Computer Festival was held in Atlantic City in September 1976.
All our work and we're stuck back here. We should be out there with the other companies.
We don't have enough money for one of those flashy booths.
APPLE
These companies are selling their computers in sleek metal cases.
NEW
The LATEST!
NEW!
Their computers have built-in keyboards and flashy designs.
That stuff takes money, too.
APPLE
Well, I guess we'll have to find a way to get some.
APPLE

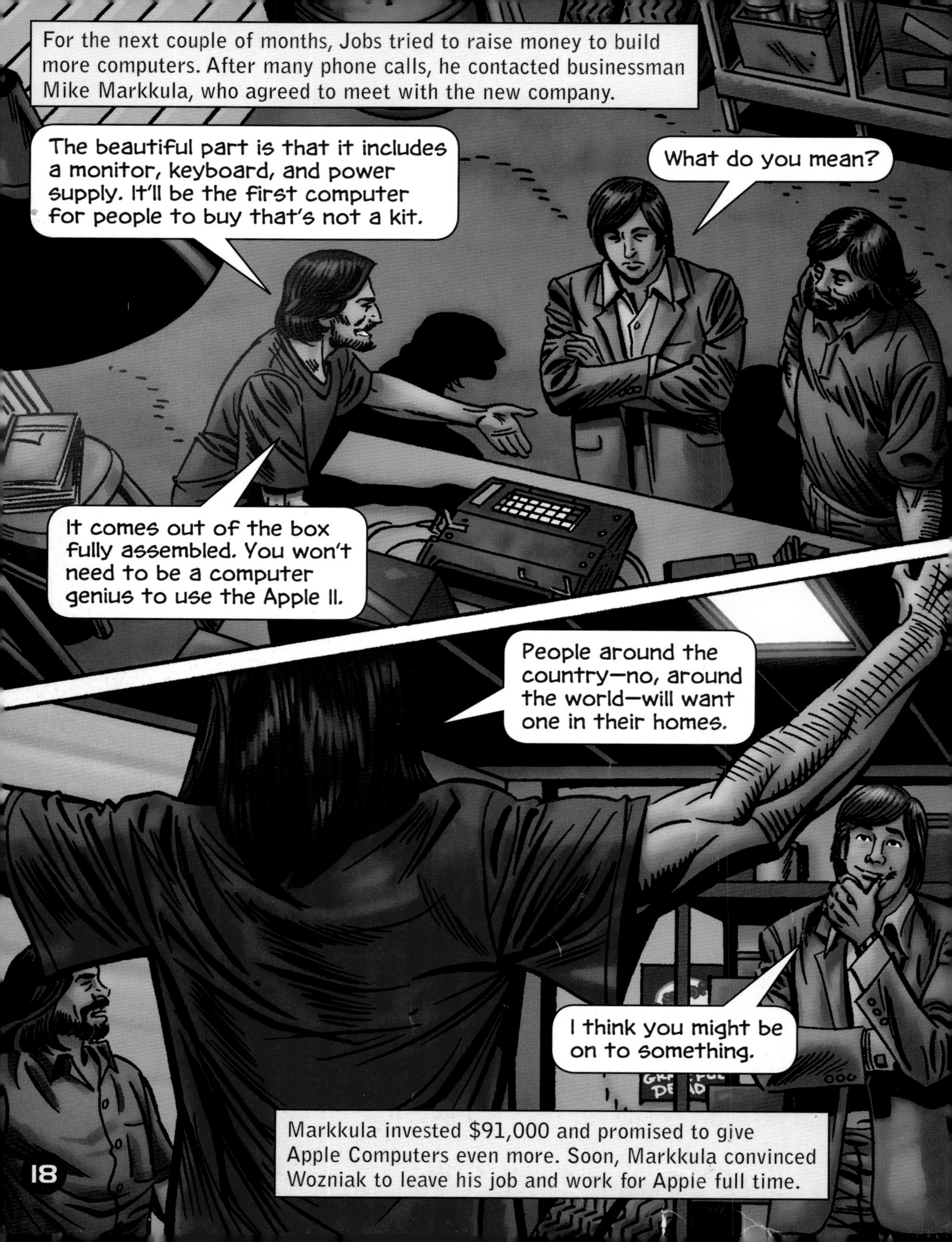
For the next couple of months, Jobs tried to raise money to build more computers. After many phone calls, he contacted businessman Mike Markkula, who agreed to meet with the new company.
The beautiful part is that it includes a monitor, keyboard, and power supply. It'll be the first computer for people to buy that's not a kit.
What do you mean?
It comes out of the box fully assembled. You won't need to be a computer genius to use the Apple II.
People around the country—no, around the world—will want one in their homes.
I think you might be on to something.
Markkula invested $91,000 and promised to give Apple Computers even more. Soon, Markkula convinced Wozniak to leave his job and work for Apple full time.

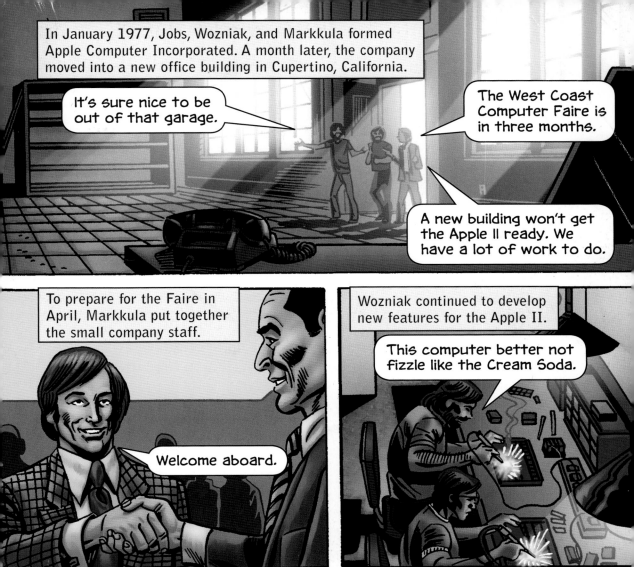

In January 1977, Jobs, Wozniak, and Markkula formed Apple Computer Incorporated. A month later, the company moved into a new office building in Cupertino, California.

It's sure nice to be out of that garage.

The West Coast Computer Faire is in three months.

A new building won't get the Apple II ready. We have a lot of work to do.

To prepare for the Faire in April, Markkula put together the small company staff.

Welcome aboard.

Wozniak continued to develop new features for the Apple II.

This computer better not fizzle like the Cream Soda.

Meanwhile, Jobs helped create a new corporate logo.

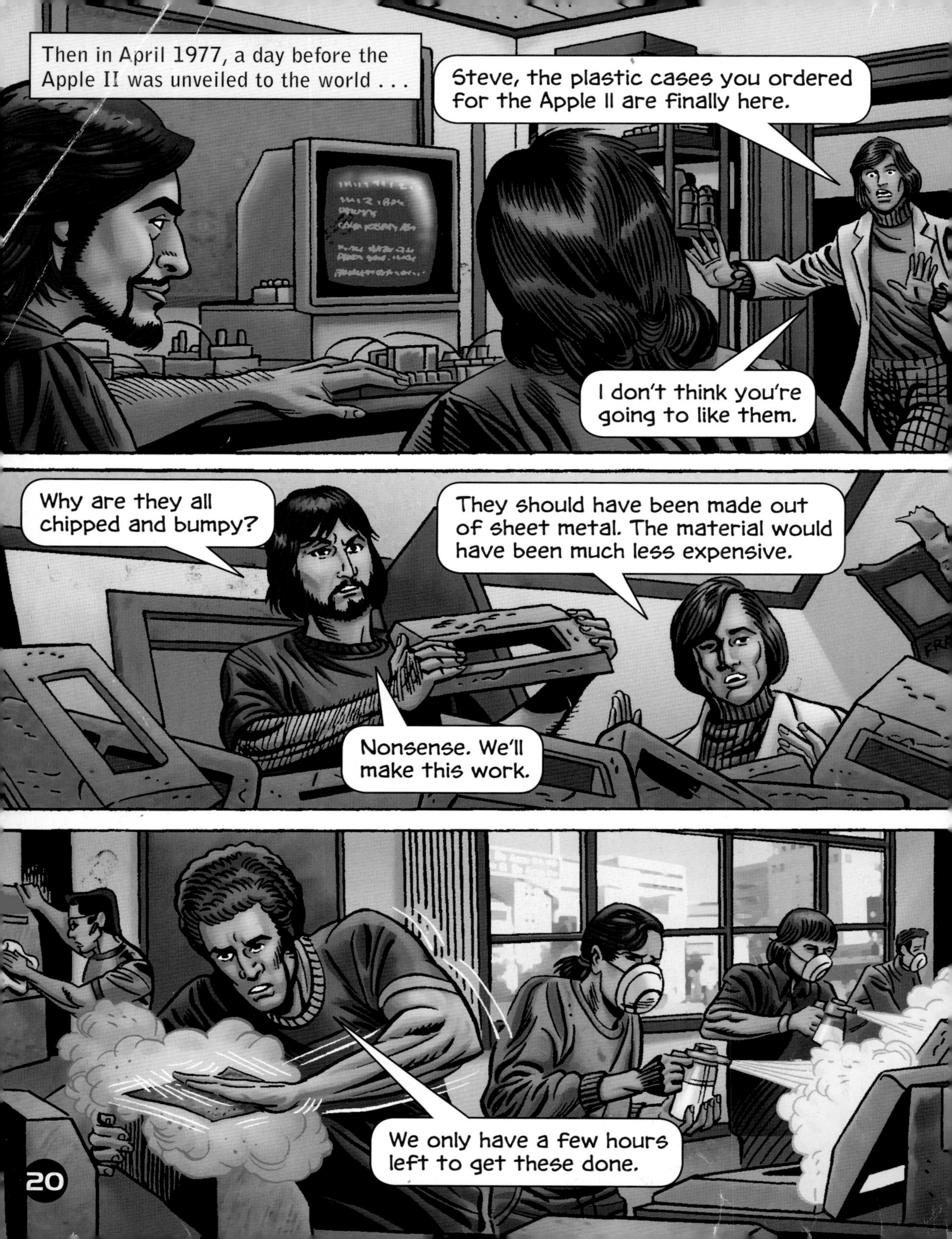
Then in April 1977, a day before the Apple II was unveiled to the world . . .
Steve, the plastic cases you ordered for the Apple II are finally here.
I don't think you're going to like them.
Why are they all chipped and bumpy?
They should have been made out of sheet metal. The material would have been much less expensive.
Nonsense. We'll make this work.
We only have a few hours left to get these done.

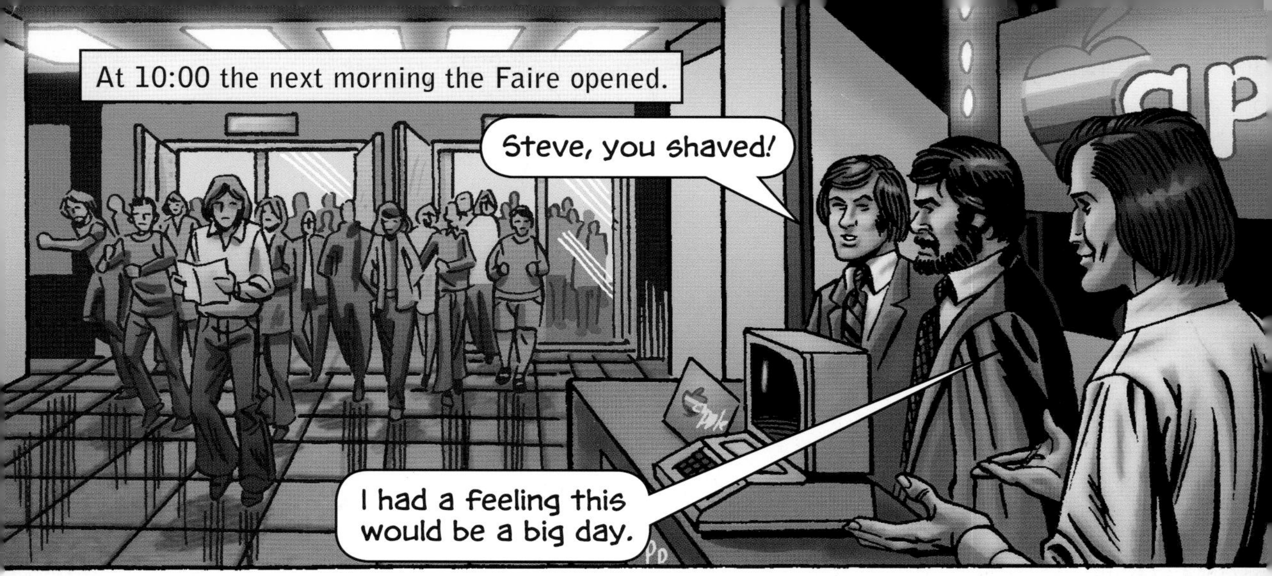
At 10:00 the next morning the Faire opened.
Steve, you shaved!
I had a feeling this would be a big day.

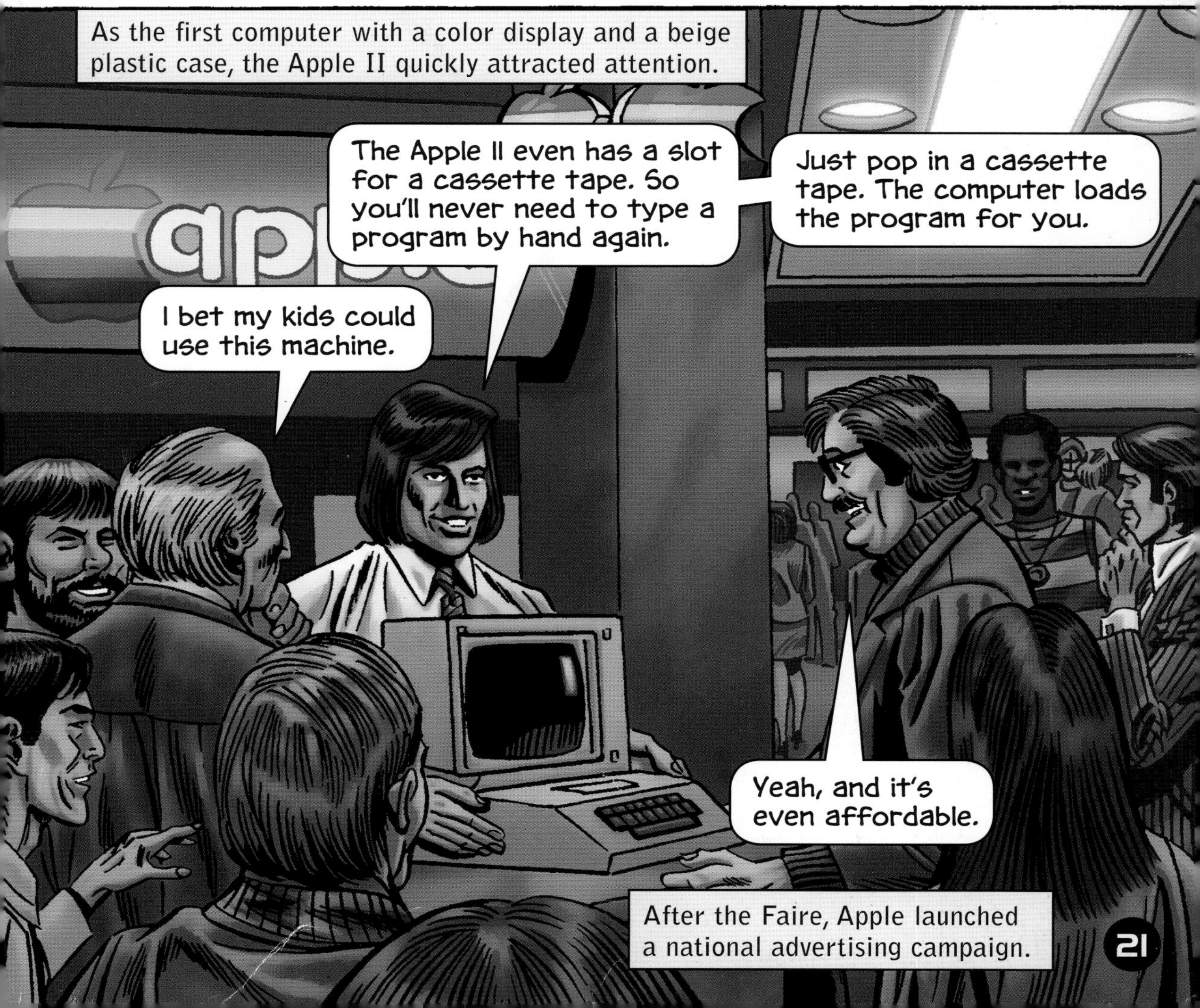
As the first computer with a color display and a beige plastic case, the Apple II quickly attracted attention.
The Apple II even has a slot for a cassette tape. So you'll never need to type a program by hand again.
Just pop in a cassette tape. The computer loads the program for you.
I bet my kids could use this machine.
Yeah, and it's even affordable.
After the Faire, Apple launched a national advertising campaign.

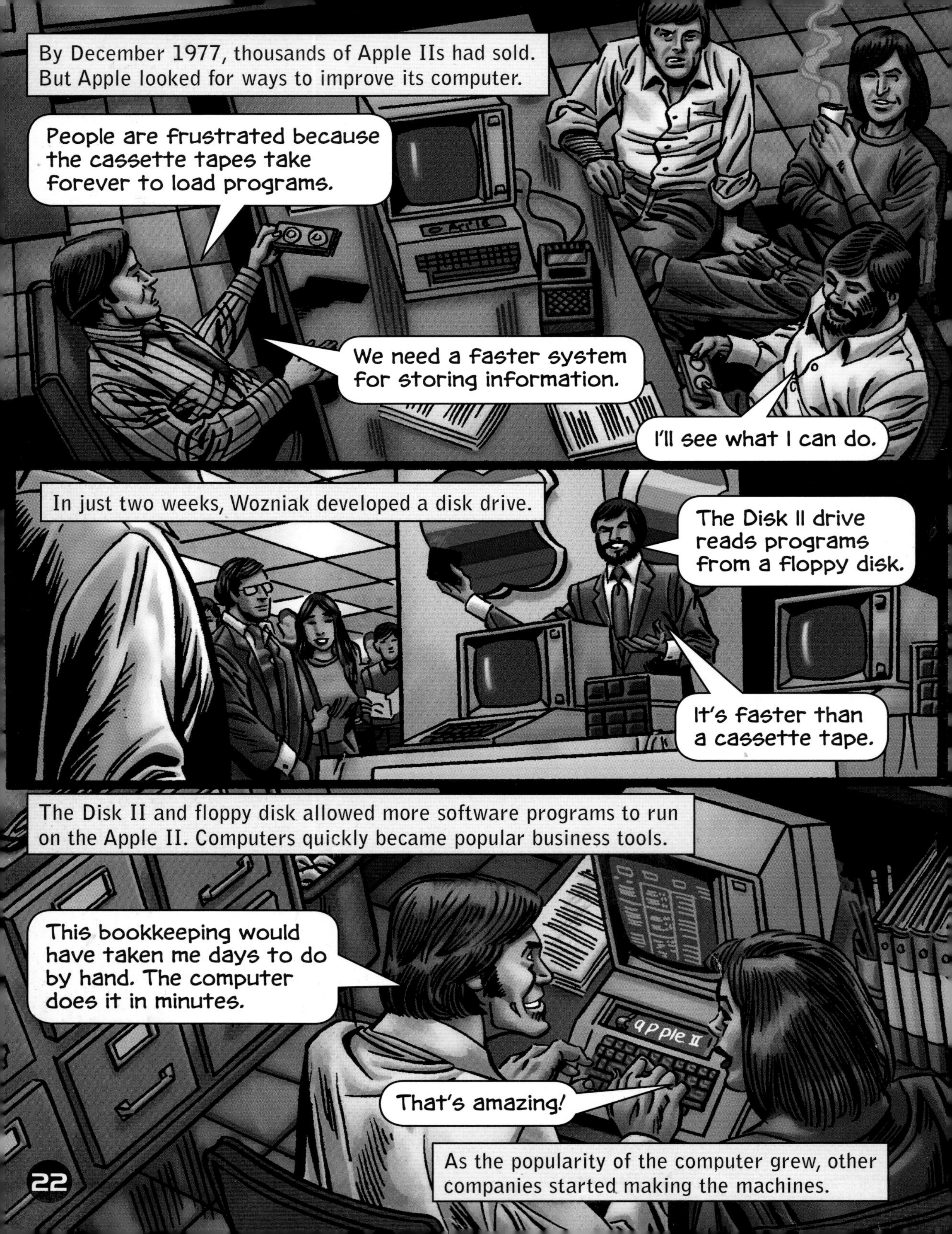
By December 1977, thousands of Apple IIs had sold. But Apple looked for ways to improve its computer.
People are frustrated because the cassette tapes take forever to load programs.
We need a faster system for storing information.
I'll see what I can do.
In just two weeks, Wozniak developed a disk drive.
The Disk II drive reads programs from a floppy disk.
It's faster than a cassette tape.
The Disk II and floppy disk allowed more software programs to run on the Apple II. Computers quickly became popular business tools.
This bookkeeping would have taken me days to do by hand. The computer does it in minutes.
apple II
That's amazing!
As the popularity of the computer grew, other companies started making the machines.

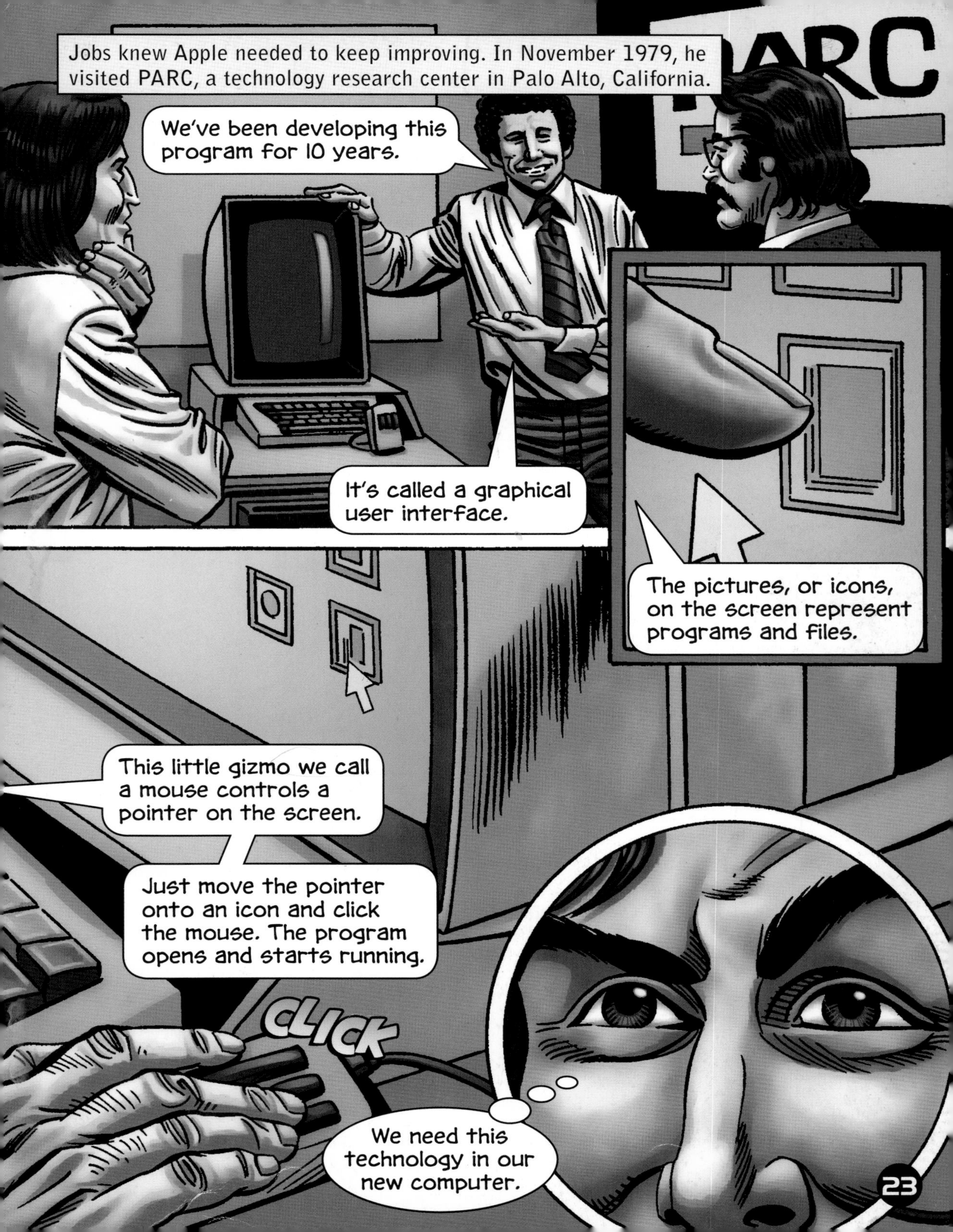
Jobs knew Apple needed to keep improving. In November 1979, he visited PARC, a technology research center in Palo Alto, California.
PARC
We've been developing this program for 10 years.
It's called a graphical user interface.
The pictures, or icons, on the screen represent programs and files.
This little gizmo we call a mouse controls a pointer on the screen.
Just move the pointer onto an icon and click the mouse. The program opens and starts running.
CLICK
We need this technology in our new computer.

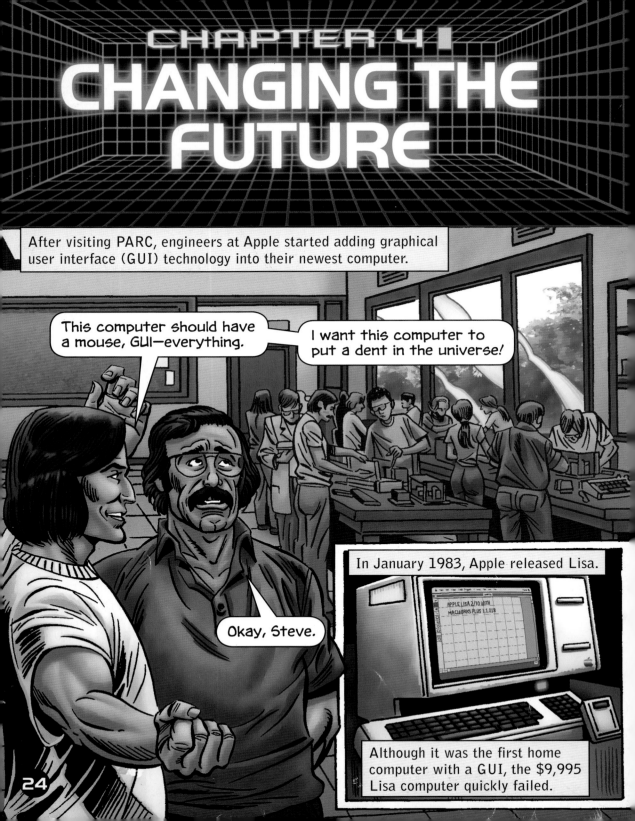

CHAPTER 4
CHANGING THE FUTURE

After visiting PARC, engineers at Apple started adding graphical user interface (GUI) technology into their newest computer.

This computer should have a mouse, GUI—everything.

I want this computer to put a dent in the universe!

Okay, Steve.

In January 1983, Apple released Lisa.

Although it was the first home computer with a GUI, the $9,995 Lisa computer quickly failed.

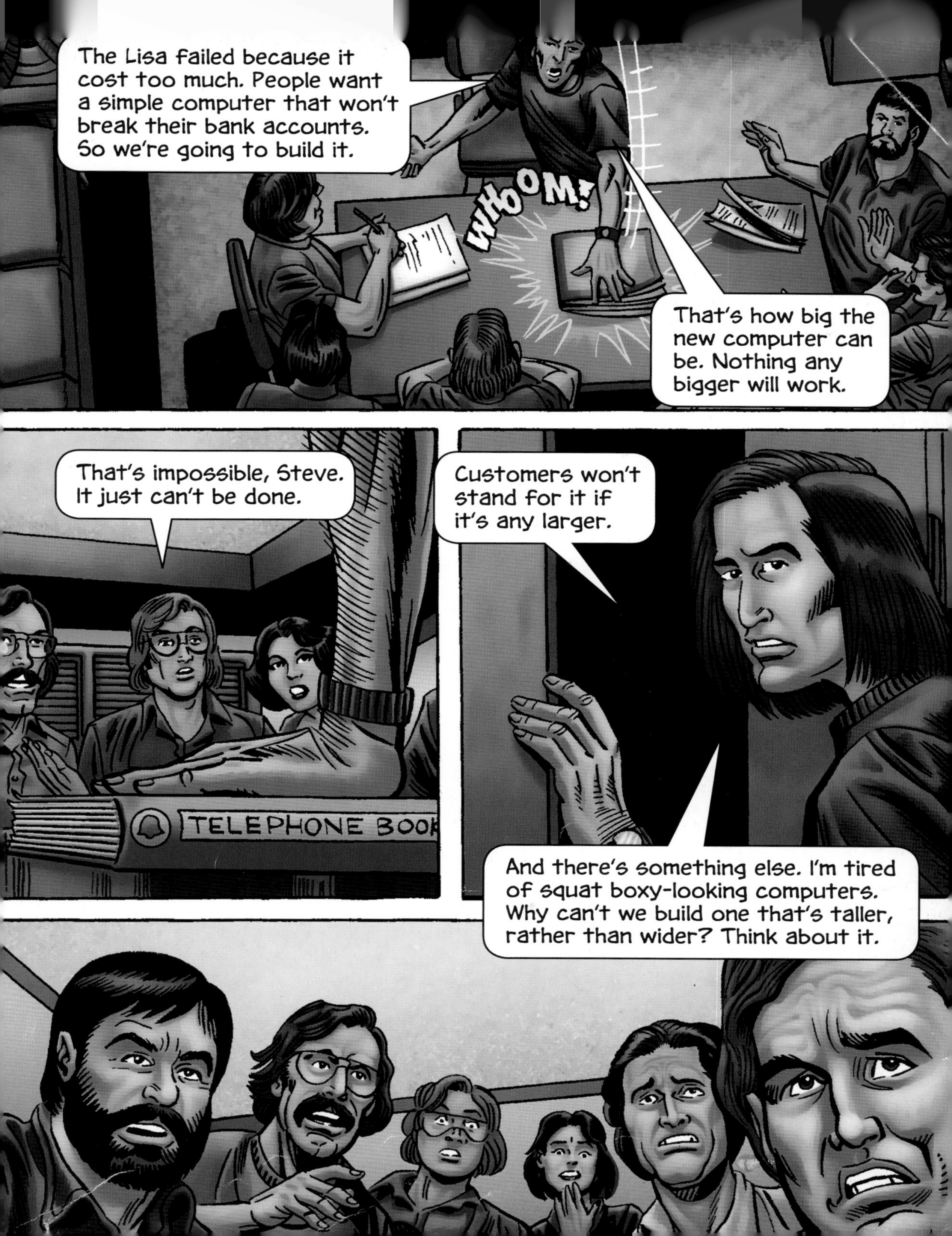
The Lisa failed because it cost too much. People want a simple computer that won't break their bank accounts. So we're going to build it.
WHOOM!
That's how big the new computer can be. Nothing any bigger will work.
That's impossible, Steve. It just can't be done.
TELEPHONE BOOK
Customers won't stand for it if it's any larger.
And there's something else. I'm tired of squat boxy-looking computers. Why can't we build one that's taller, rather than wider? Think about it.

On January 24, 1984, Apple Computer and Steve Jobs amazed the world.

I'd like to introduce to you the computer of the future.

SHUNGKK

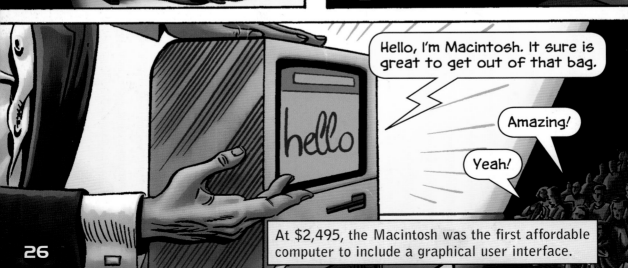

hello

Hello, I'm Macintosh. It sure is great to get out of that bag.

Amazing!

Yeah!

At $2,495, the Macintosh was the first affordable computer to include a graphical user interface.

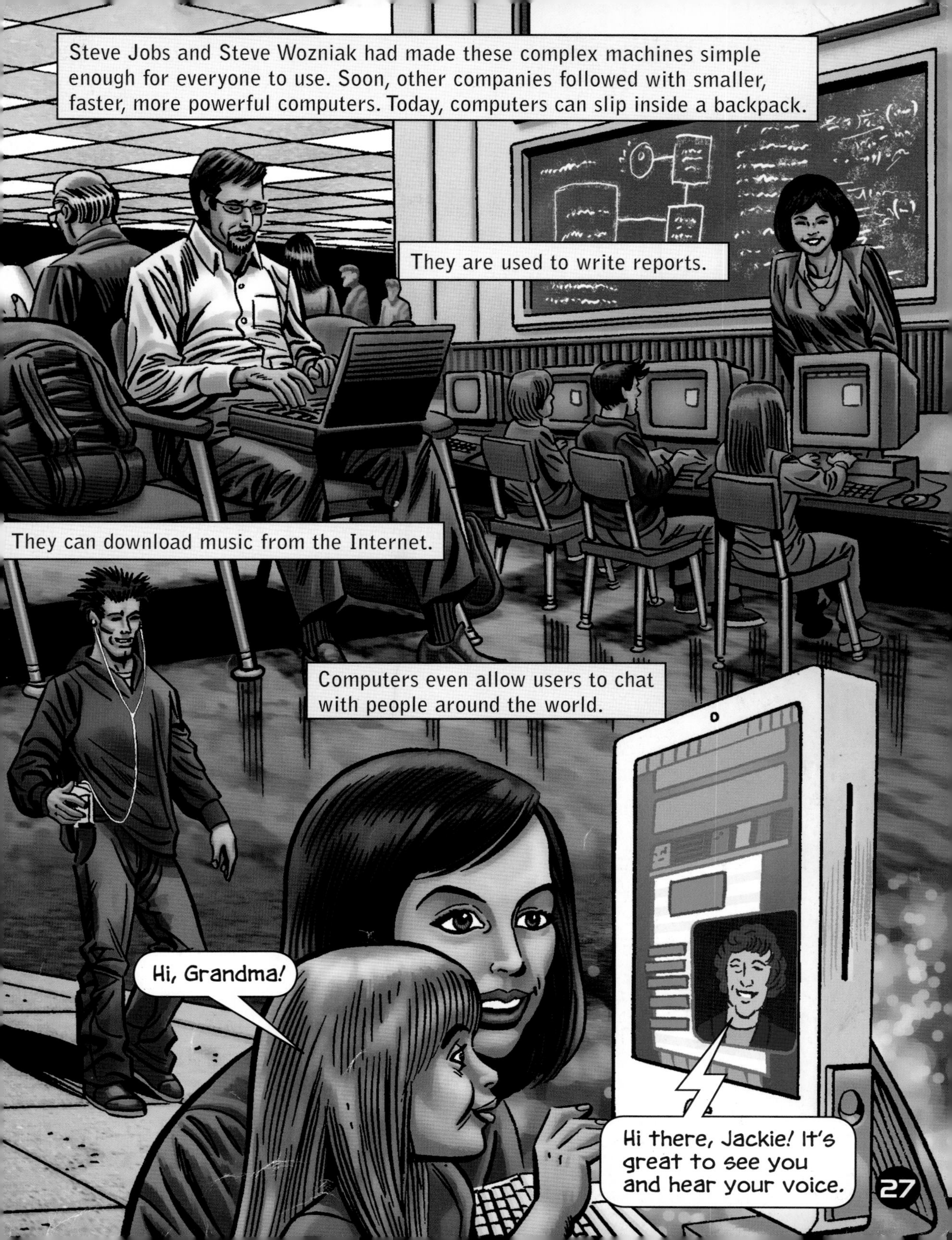
Steve Jobs and Steve Wozniak had made these complex machines simple enough for everyone to use. Soon, other companies followed with smaller, faster, more powerful computers. Today, computers can slip inside a backpack.
They are used to write reports.
They can download music from the Internet.
Computers even allow users to chat with people around the world.
Hi, Grandma!
Hi there, Jackie! It's great to see you and hear your voice.

MORE ABOUT
JOBS, WOZNIAK, AND THE
PERSONAL COMPUTER

- Steve Wozniak was born in San Jose, California, on August 11, 1950. His parents encouraged their son's interest in electronics from an early age. By the sixth grade, Wozniak had built a computer that could play a tic-tac-toe game.

- Steve Jobs was born in San Francisco, California, on February 24, 1955. He grew up in an area of California now known as Silicon Valley.

- In the early 1970s, Silicon Valley became the nickname for the area south of San Francisco. This region has many computer companies, including Apple Computer Inc. Silicon Valley got is name from the microprocessors inside computers that are made from a material called silicon.

- Atari paid Jobs $1,000 for designing the video game Breakout. Jobs had promised to split the money with Wozniak, but he kept $700 for himself. Years later, Wozniak found out, and the unfair split damaged their friendship.

No one knows for sure where Jobs and Wozniak came up with their company's name. Some people believe Jobs named the company Apple because he once worked on a Colorado apple orchard. Others believe the name honors their favorite rock 'n' roll group, the Beatles. The group owned a company called Apple Records.

During the 1970s and 1980s, many other companies were building and selling microcomputers. In 1981, International Business Machines (IBM) released the IBM PC. Many believe it was the first machine to be labeled a "personal computer."

On February 19, 1985, Wozniak and Jobs received the National Medal of Technology from President Ronald Reagan. This award is the highest honor given to American innovators.

Today, Steve Wozniak is a leading member of two successful technology companies. He also enjoys teaching students about computers. Steve Jobs continues to head Apple Computer Inc. He is also a leader at Pixar Animation Studios and Walt Disney Company. Pixar created computer-animated films such as *Toy Story*, *Finding Nemo*, *The Incredibles,* and *Cars*.

GLOSSARY

circuit board (SUR-kit BORD)—a thin plate inside a computer on which chips and other electronic components are placed

graphical user interface (GUI) (GRAF-ik-uhl YOOZ-uhr IN-tur-fayss)—a program that allows users to control a computer with windows, pull-down menus, clickable buttons, scroll bars, icons, and images instead of complex commands

microprocessor (MYE-kroh-prah-sess-uhr)—a silicon chip inside a computer that contains the central processing unit (CPU); the central processing unit is where most of the computer's calculations take place.

minicomputer (MIN-ee-kuhm-pyoo-tur)—a computer between a microcomputer and a mainframe in size, speed, and capacity; minicomputers were about the size of a refrigerator.

INTERNET SITES

FactHound offers a safe, fun way to find Internet sites related to this book. All of the sites on FactHound have been researched by our staff.

Here's how:
1. Visit *www.facthound.com*
2. Choose your grade level.
3. Type in this book ID **0736864881** for age-appropriate sites. You may also browse subjects by clicking on letters, or by clicking on pictures and words.
4. Click on the **Fetch It** button.

FactHound will fetch the best sites for you!

READ MORE

Brackett, Virginia. *Steve Jobs: Computer Genius of Apple.* Internet Biographies. Berkeley Heights, N.J.: Enslow, 2003.

Brashares, Ann. *Steve Jobs: Thinks Different.* Techies. Brookfield, Conn.: Twenty-First Century Books, 2001.

Riddle, John, and Jim Whiting. *Stephen Wozniak and the Story of Apple Computer.* Unlocking the Secrets of Science. Bear, Del.: Mitchell Lane, 2002.

Worland, Gayle. *The Computer.* Great Inventions. Mankato, Minn.: Capstone Press, 2004.

BIBLIOGRAPHY

Deutschman, Alan. *The Second Coming of Steve Jobs.* New York: Broadway Books, 2000.

Freiberger, Paul, and Michael Swaine. *Fire in the Valley: The Making of the Personal Computer.* New York: McGraw-Hill, 2000.

Mac Essentials. *It's great to get out of that bag.* http://www.mac-essentials.de/index.php/mac/14276.

Woz.org. *The Official Website of Steve Wozniak.* http://www.woz.org.

Young, Jeffrey S., and William L. Simon. *iCon: Steve Jobs, The Greatest Second Act in the History of Business.* Hoboken, N.J.: Wiley, 2005.

INDEX